MATTERS
of the
HEART

MATTERS *of the* HEART

8 KEYS TO PRACTICING SELF-LOVE

LINDA G. HODGE

KP PUBLISHING COMPANY

Copyright 2021 by Linda G. Hodge
All rights reserved. In accordance with the U.S. Copyright Act of 1976, the scanning, uploading, and electronic sharing of any part of this book without the permission of the publisher is unlawful piracy and theft of the author's intellectual property. If you would like to use material from this book (other than for review purposes), prior written permission must be obtained by contacting the publisher at info@knowledgepowerinc.com.

Thank you for your support of the author's rights.
ISBN: 978-1-950936-65-6 (Paperback)
ISBN: 978-1-950936-66-3 (Ebook)
Library of Congress Control Number:

Editor: Penny Scott
Cover Design: Angie Alaya
Interior Design: Jennifer Houle
Ebook: Ashley Merritt
Literary Director: Sandra Slayton James

Published by:

KP Publishing Company
Publisher of Fiction, Nonfiction & Children's Books
Valencia, CA 91355
www.kp-pub.com

Printed in the United States of America

CONTENTS

Introduction ix

Chapter 1	Let Go of Excuses	1
Chapter 2	Change Your Thinking	7
Chapter 3	Make an Attitude Shift	11
Chapter 4	Make a Heart Adjustment	15
Chapter 5	Love Yourself	23
Chapter 6	Embrace God's Love	35
Chapter 7	Discover Your Best	47
Chapter 8	Get Out of Your Feelings	57

Emotional Capacity Questions 65
About the Author 67

INTRODUCTION

How many of you have heard the phrase, "I believe in you, but do you believe in you?" The ability to believe in yourself is one of the most important qualities a person can have. Possessing the confidence of believing in yourself is really not something you acquire. It's already inside of you.

Everyone was born with all the confidence and self-esteem they need. Any doubts, judgments or fears you have about yourself were learned over time—they are not truths that should be valued. These "false fears" are merely mental constructs.

In this book, we will be discussing "Matters of the Heart" and what it means to "believe in yourself" in order to Practice Self-Love. Knowing how to love and protect yourself is a priceless treasure—that's waiting to be discovered. And this treasure is buried deep underneath trauma, learned behaviors, self-doubt, and low self-esteem. Time to pull your "kid gloves off," put on your hard hat, and grab your excavation tools. Let's "pan for gold" and find buried treasure.

MATTERS of the HEART

CHAPTER ONE
LET GO OF EXCUSES

"Digging for unknown riches is hard work. Beneath the dirt, the closely packed rocks are heavy with iron ore. Some are sharp, and when uncovered, they threaten to make one bleed if not handled correctly. But you never know what you may find in all the rubble. One must be willing to keep digging, despite the exhaustion. It's like having your body filled with sandstone. Every part of your body is extremely heavy and hard to move—including your eyelids, which become difficult to keep open. Excuses overshadow unknown riches . . . Beneath the dirt, rocks, and waste, hidden treasures are ready to emerge. Dirt doesn't have to signify the end. But the exit of one thing is always the beginning of something new. The Bible says, "Then the Lord God formed a man from the dust of the ground and breathed into his nostrils the breath of life, and the man became a living being."

—Linda G. Hodge

An excuse is simply a state of not wanting to put in the work to overcome a hurdle in your life. Excuses are fake news that we piled together in our mind. Such excuses have no true value or authenticity. It's funny how we get extremely defensive about our excuses. It's because excuses free us from taking responsibility for our lives. We say things like, "I didn't get fired because I lost my temper. I got fired because my boss is too sensitive." Excuses are usually tied up in a pretty package, with a bright glittery bow. They're our "get out of reality card." All I have to do is pull the card whenever I'm faced with the situation of not having an answer, or not wanting to

Let Go of Excuses

tell the truth. Some people live their whole lives making excuses, while others use it only as an "emergency card" for threatening conditions. Excuses are designed for our comfort zones—staying in situations too long, then straying out into unknown territory. Besides, most of us don't want to go where we've never gone before. Unknown territories are usually risky but necessary. Furthermore, in many circumstances, excuses require a change of thinking, an attitude shift, a heart adjustment, and a whole lot of courage.

Sally had come to the end of her rope and made a decision that she no longer wanted to live a life of excuses. She knew it would take a tremendous amount of soul-searching on her part. In 2007, she had been in a terrible car accident. Sally remembers being pulled out of her car with her blouse on fire and learned afterward that her legs were broken in seven places. During the recovery, she reflected on her life and discovered that she didn't particularly care about living. Sally experienced third-degree burns and the excruciating pain she experienced during the healing process was unbearable and unbelievable at times. The broken bones in Sally's legs were equally painful. To Sally, living life in a leg cast for eight months seemed unfair. The idea of asking others to help was equally embarrassing.

Waking each morning only to remain seated throughout the day in a wheelchair was mentally excruciating for Sally. Enduring the seven-month process of healing seemed like an eternity. Watching the clock tick-tock every second throughout the day was draining the hope of living a full, productive life.

Excuses of getting back in shape again were tormenting Sally. The thoughts of not returning back to work again were looking more appealing. It seemed easier to make excuses for not pursuing her once before desire of living life to the fullest. Due to Sally's mentally and physically painful process of healing, she often "convinced herself" it was easier to settle with the idea of living a physically disabled life.

But then, Sally reached an epiphany. She decided to pull the excuse bag off her shoulders. Her shoulders had become tired of carrying the heavy load of excuses. Seemingly, the excuses were multiplying and got heavier by the day. A change of thinking, an attitude shift, a heart adjustment, and a big, heaping jar of courage was the formula Sally needed to rise from her dilemma. She knew the road ahead would be difficult, but it was more frightening to remain in her "comfort zone of excuses."

So, Sally put one foot forward, "looking to Jesus as the Author and Finisher of her faith."

CHAPTER TWO
CHANGE YOUR THINKING

"There's a kind of weariness that requires a good night's sleep and another kind of exhaustion that needs so much more. When you are drenched in sweat, and your muscles are experiencing pure fatigue, it's like wearing a jacket filled with weights. There is a certain level of weariness that equates to insanity, or "drunk-driving your life." At the height of your frustrating search for buried treasures, your brain is barely functioning at a five percent battery rate. You begin feeling extremely depleted, limp, dispirited, and no longer want to continue searching for unknown treasures."

—Linda G. Hodge

Sally jump-started her internal transformation by changing her thought process. She had read that repeating affirmations would be essential in her "excuse recovery." Sally began placing Post-it Notes all over her house. The positive affirmations said thoughts such as, "I am special. I am loved. I am worthy." And, frantically going from room to room ripping them down when you realize your friends are at the door is so worth the risk.

Affirmations are used to reprogram the subconscious mind, to encourage us to believe certain things about ourselves. They are also used to help us create the reality we want. An affirmation opens the door. Our belief in the affirmation seals the deal! These faith-filled words will either eliminate something from your life or help create something new in your life.

Every thought you think and every word you speak is an affirmation, whether negative or positive. All of our self-talk and internal dialogue is a stream of affirmations or confessions. You're using affirmations every moment whether you know it or not. You're affirming and creating your life experiences with every word and thought.

Your beliefs are merely habitual thinking patterns that you learned as a child. During childhood, did you have a teacher who constantly belittled you? Did that teacher praise everyone around you but never mentioned your good deeds? Maybe, it was a parent who never fostered your gift of art, music, sewing, or cooking. Those young years are so impactful, they leave a lasting impression on your soul. Beliefs of doubt or uncertainty may be limiting your ability to create the very things you say you want. What you want and what you believe you deserve may be very different.

Every time you get angry, you're affirming that you want more anger in your life. Every time you feel like a victim, you're affirming that you want to continue to feel like a victim. If you feel that God doesn't want the best for your life, then you are robbing yourself of God's best for your life. It is time for us to create the life we want by affirming and confessing what the Word of God says about us.

So, where do you start? The best place it to begin by writing confessions/affirmations that you know you need to implement in your life. For example, if you know you need to eliminate excuses from your life, then begin writing a confession similar to this: Father, I thank You that excuses are no longer part of my existence. Therefore, I will no longer make excuses for my behavior, for my actions, for my thoughts, for my health and wellness, etc.

CHAPTER THREE
MAKE AN ATTITUDE SHIFT

"In traditional surface and underground mining, hammers and chisels with pickaxes and shovels are used. Minecarts move ore and other materials during mining. Pans are used for placer mining operations, such as gold panning. Each tool has a designated purpose for a designated outcome. Without the proper tool, you won't achieve the desired result. Some tools are made only for right and left-hand handlers. A particular tool is crafted for a specific dig. Using the wrong tool will not penetrate the ground effectively. You may have some success, but not optimal success.

Therefore, using the proper tool yields a greater harvest of productivity with less strain and struggle."

—Linda G. Hodge

Your attitude is the next battle you need to conquer. Everything in our "reality" is reflected back to us, depending on how we choose to perceive it. A bad attitude stems from perception. Some perceptions bear facts, but no truth. There is a huge difference between facts vs. truth. It may be a fact that someone doesn't like you. But the truth of the matter is them not liking you does not define you! My attitude either adds fuel to the fire or extinguishes the fire. The enemy is always looking to fuel the fire at any given moment. And he uses our attitude to flame the fire. A harsh word, a dirty look, or a disingenuous disposition toward us are like fiery sparks that cause the flame to rise.

One of the quickest ways to test your attitude is to answer this question: "Do you feel your world is fair? "When you feel the world is not fair to you then you will see everything from a negative lens. We are individually responsible for our view of life.

Make an Attitude Shift

"Whatever a man sows, this he will also reap."
Galatians 6:7 (KJV)

Negative talking is contagious, it blows everything out of proportion, and negative thinking limits God and our potential. One of the saddest stories in the Bible is about Israel's failure to enter the promised land as told in Numbers 13 and 14.

Twelve spies went into Canaan under the same orders, to the same places, at the same time and came back with different advice. For Joshua and Caleb, the promised land was everything that God said it would be. They reported, "It certainly does flow with milk and honey and this is its fruit."

The other ten men offered a negative report. In verses 28 and 29 of chapter 13, they reported facts without faith. How many times do we choose to believe the opposite of what God says to us? And as a result, we shortchange ourselves because of our estimation of how we view ourselves.

Most of the prison bars we beat against are within us; we put them there and we can take them down. To work toward believing in yourself, you may want to consider the process of overcoming an attitude problem. However, the process takes a lot of dedication and work to be effective. The process of change is never complete, therefore constant review will ensure the best results. All excuses for wrong attitudes must be eliminated immediately. Face-changing negative attitudes with the old spiritual, "It's me, it's me, it's me, oh Lord, standing in the need of prayer." Then, find a friend to whom you can be accountable on a regular basis for your change of attitude. As you learn more about Christ, submit to His will and obey His leading, your bitterness toward life changes. Life becomes a blessing, not a burden. Life becomes full of opportunities, not obstacles.

There are no stressful situations—only stressful ways of perceiving situations, and blessed you are in control of your thoughts. The next time a challenging situation presents itself; take a pause and make the conscious choice to meet it with humor or the knowledge that this, too, shall pass. You have nothing to gain by freaking out.

CHAPTER FOUR
MAKE A HEART ADJUSTMENT

"The '49ers Gold Rush People dreamed of a better life for their families. In pursuit of a better life for their families, these miners were willing to travel great distances away from their families and brave harsh weather conditions. Because of their expectation, the dream was something far off in their minds yet near in the distance. Inadvertently, from time-to-time, they must have become weary while digging. Wondering "when am I going to strike gold." I can imagine they must have felt like giving up on many occasions. Rehearsing in their minds, "was the trip worth the dig?" Others with low self-confidence would unconsciously sabotage their dig, feeling unworthy of receiving God's best and abundance. Consequently, in their minds, stopping and aborting the mission would have been much easier to do than remaining persistent. They failed to realize the same God who stepped out of nothing, into nothing, and stood on nothing, with nothing, and created everything is the God who dwells in them by the power of His Holy Spirit."

—Linda G. Hodge

Sometimes, we hold stuff against ourselves. We blame ourselves for not making the right decision or choosing the wrong path. It's time to choose the path to freedom. You have to give yourself permission to hold space in your heart for that dream and to dream bigger and believe beyond where you are. Oftentimes, you are fighting against yourself. Some have held their pain so close to their heart, that it has hidden their purpose. Unconsciously, we tend to carry illusions in our hearts about ourselves

Make a Heart Adjustment

that can block our confidence. This, in turn, can short circuit our relationships, and even our health.

Untangling from illusions of the past can give you a different perspective and help you see the water in which you're swimming. Some of us are swimming in polluted water because we have allowed our hearts to be defiled by ourselves. The good news is that you can untangle yourself from a hardened heart toward yourself and unleash your "hidden" confidence. It has been hiding because it is afraid to be vulnerable to self. Holding onto anger and resentment is an internal issue. When we harbor unresolved feelings, especially about ourselves, we literally turn them inward upon ourselves, where they ravage the nervous, digestive, cardiac and respiratory systems.

Sometimes to get your life back, you have to face the death of what you thought your life would look like. It's our choice whether we stay stuck in our hurt or get renewed in our hearts.

Courage is crucial for everyone. Many people have beautiful, life-transforming dreams and ideas that they have been unable to realize due to lack of courage.

MATTERS OF THE HEART

Courage is essential in believing in yourself. Courage gives you the confidence to declare the ability of your God and enjoy His unfailing covenant promises. It is courage that enables you to act on the Word.

Simply defined, courage is an untiring and undefeated attitude, born out of determination. It is basically an issue of the heart. Courage is not subject to the environment, neither does it cower to public opinion.

Courage is the ability to retain your language even when circumstances pressure you to change. When you possess courage, nothing will be able to intimidate you. A woman or man of courage neither requires outside support nor inspiration to keep going. He is naturally motivated.

Every courageous step has some degree of risk attached to it. If you are waiting for risk-free moments, you will never move.

Every move into a higher phase of life involves sacrifice, which is also a risk born out of courage.

Courage is a force. It compels the ground to open up to you. Only people of courage are sensitive to opportunities.

Make a Heart Adjustment

When you are approaching a battle, one thing you need for success is a reflection on past victories. Sit down and write out your past victories; thank God for them, and tell Him that you are sure He will give you yet another victory. Testimonies are powerful weapons for turning the switch of courage on.

Self-worth enhances and helps to boost one's courage. That is, knowing yourself and your abilities, and placing a high value on them. You must see yourself the way God sees you.

> *"I can do all things through Christ which strengthens me."*
> Philippians 4:13 (KJV)

If you wait for people's assessment of your abilities, you may never do anything. How do you assess yourself? Place yourself before the mirror of God's Word. Just as the physical mirror shows you and your physical image so also does the spiritual mirror (God's Word reveals your spiritual worth and qualities).

Until you rate yourself high, people will never rate

you high. You need to make discoveries about yourself. Are you aware of the great potential and creative abilities you possess? Are you conscious of the fact that you are a product of possibility and that you carry God's nature of possibility inside you?

It is time to examine yourself because self-examination leads to self-awareness and that brings about fulfillment.

You inspire courage in yourself by placing a correct value on yourself.

> *For as he thinketh in his heart, so is he"*
> Proverbs 23:7 (KJV)

It's time to declare a good image of yourself. Bold declarations infuse and induce courage within. The more you speak, the more courageous you become. Your words are the fuel of your life. If you cannot speak, then you will be driven backward.

You will build courage by reminding yourself, "Greater is He that is in me than he that is in the world. God is for me, no man or devil can be against me," etc.

Make a Heart Adjustment

Until your mouth ceases to speak, your life will not cease to function.

Jesus is our example. He kept on making bold statements; He never stopped to apologize or explain things to His critics. Rather, He went ahead every time to announce boldly who He was. "I am the Bread of Life. Before Abraham was, I am."

Let's consider Sir Edmund Hillary, the man who climbed to the top of Mount Everest—the highest mountain in the world. Sir Edmund and his colleagues made several unsuccessful attempts at climbing the mountain. But one day, Edmund stood before the mountain and addressed it.

He said to it: "Mountain, you have overcome me till now, but no more. You have grown all that you will ever grow, but I am still growing." And in 1964, Sir Edmund stood on the mountain's summit, waving his hand to the whole world. He had overcome at last! That victory was born out of courage.

Many people might have stood at the base of the mountain and asked, "Who will ever make it to the top?" But Sir Edmund derived encouragement from the same circumstance that left many discouraged. The difference between him and the others was his disposition. He provoked courage by magnifying his self-worth over the frightening height of the mountain.

> *"For assuredly, I say to you,*
> *whoever says to this mountain*
> *Be removed and be cast into the sea,*
> *and does not doubt in His heart,*
> *but believes that those things*
> *he says will be done,*
> *He will whatever he says."*
> Mark 11:23 (NKJ)

CHAPTER FIVE
LOVE YOURSELF

"There are countless stories of those who experienced death on the journey to reach California in search of gold. Disease and death was rampant as miners strived to make the long haul in pursuit of wealth. Inevitably, they had to face anxiety in a way that shut down the chatter and inner voices telling them they couldn't make it. They fought hard against the voice of fear—that devious little voice pollutes inner confidence by whispering doubt and worry. That voice is a master at invading our hearts and hijacking our minds with disbelief.

How many times have you given up on your dream, your passion, your gift, and your purpose?

Not realizing you were closer than you thought. It's time to emerge, which means to come into view, become visible, make an appearance. You emerge by giving yourself permission to love yourself."

—Linda G. Hodge

Loving yourself is one of the basic fundamental things one can do. Loving yourself unleashes a person's worth which ignites a boomeranging effect that touches the core of a person's existence. It releases a limitless reservoir of peace. True peace comes from who you really are. When you choose to love yourself, you have tapped into your innate strength and essence of who you are as a human being. Maybe, we all need to develop a whole new mindset that is 100 percent centered around all we have to offer to humanity. Maybe, we need to dwell in our strength and power instead of our liabilities.

Loving yourself may resemble; anticipating a new life, your new normal.

Loving yourself may resemble; knowing that you can choose how to show up in life.

Love Yourself

Loving yourself may resemble; giving yourself permission to be creative and do what you really want to do. You "show up" as your authentic self—not what people expect of you based on their previous encounters with you.

Loving yourself may resemble; shifting your priorities to facilitate growth and expansion. Loving yourself may resemble; giving yourself more grace to run your own race.

Loving yourself may resemble; giving yourself permission to have adventure and spontaneity.

Peace is our power and peace is a new success. We have spent countless hours chasing a dream or career that is now a tiny spark that is growing dim by the hour. They have spent thousands of dollars attaining an education to finally realize that the once desired goal is non-recognizable.

Contrary to the common misconception that loving yourself equates to being self-absorbed and lacking empathy or consideration for others, the true meaning of self-love is about caring, respecting, and knowing yourself. Self-love is about taking responsibility for your life and ultimately, your happiness.

MATTERS OF THE HEART

Loving yourself starts with liking yourself. Have you ever walked by the mirror and refused to not look at your reflection? Not wanting to be reminded of the extra 10 pounds that somehow miraculously slid on your body from just breathing air? Or possibly, that particular day you didn't resemble the perfect digital picture of yourself? Do you actually look like that "Facebook-altered" picture that makes you look 10 years younger?

Others don't necessarily avoid the mirror. Instead, they stand there, staring at the mirror. Hating what they see, and hating the girl staring back. She was broken, afraid and alone. She didn't know what the future would hold. She had spent so much of life being independent, being so sure of her own ego.

External success feeds the ego and makes it stronger and stronger. It wants to live in full view of the world to see how all together we have it. Instead of having a "reality check" of how depleted we really are. Our love tank for ourselves is empty.

That girl that everyone else saw was not the girl that was there in the mirror. That girl had begun to lose sight of herself. That girl began to have pent-up resentment, frustration, and inescapable pain. She was

Love Yourself

self-destructing and struggling to stop self-sabotage. She wonders, "How could I love this broken being?"

We all must love ourselves and be the hero of our own story. If you are not the hero of your own story, then you're missing the whole point of God's intention for you.

If you're wondering what your purpose is here on earth, I can give you the answer. You are here to find yourself. To be an expression of God Himself. To embrace yourself. To be yourself. And in order to do all of that, you must love yourself.

You see, at some point, we all experience a pivotal moment in our lives that has such a devastating effect we lose the sense of our own worth.

For me, it happened quite early. When I look back now, I can see that I lacked self-love from around the age of 13. That was shortly after my Father passed. The years that followed were tumultuous as I stripped away my true self and became less and less 'me' until I reached my early twenties and there wasn't much left of me.

Prior to starting the process of self-love, I had no idea that I was sabotaging myself so badly. If you would have asked me back then if I loved myself, I would have answered "yes." But the truth was that I was battering myself from head-to-toe every day of my life.

"I can't do that! I'm not good enough. I wish I were better." I constantly repeated phrases that limited my life and made me believe that I was less than others. I didn't deserve to expect God's best for my life.

Does any of this sound familiar?

When I began learning about self-love, I was amazed to discover that people who seemed to have it together, dress the part, speak with confidence but are hiding from their own truth.

It's usually when someone comes to the end of one's self, that she begins to reinvent herself.

The truth of the matter is the way out of self-sabotage is self-love. But, you don't need to hit rock bottom to gain self-love. You just need to stop beating yourself up mentally.

The aim is to reach a place where you like being you, where you embrace yourself, abilities, and liabilities. Once you are now comfortable with who you are, you don't look at others and feel less than them. And, you won't desire to tear yourself down at every given opportunity.

Love Yourself

When you love who you are, you will begin to learn that what you have to offer the world is significant. You'll see potential in what the world has to offer you. You'll also notice that your dreams start becoming a reality as your belief and vision for yourself continues to grow.

All challenges can be seen as a call to shift from seemingly difficult obstacles to reaching victorious outcomes. A positive mindset transforms old, limiting beliefs to mountain moving beliefs that ultimately change the trajectory of one's life.

Self-love must be a lifelong commitment.

If you want to achieve greatness, you have to love yourself first. You are the epicenter. You are everything. You have a spouse, friends, and kids, and they are all important. You receive love from them, and that's great. But, you have to love yourself before you can use that sense of worth to help others cultivate their own self-love.

And, above all else, you have to love yourself before you can help yourself. If you don't love yourself, how can you help yourself achieve your dreams? Start by spending quality time with yourself. Take one hour per day—or even half an hour, if that's all you can commit to at the start. Spend time with yourself. For example, go to a place where you can be alone and experience what it's like to just be with yourself, quietly and honestly.

Try this simple exercise. Practice it and see how you feel after you finish. Speak out loud to yourself and tell yourself great things. Repeat them over and over again. Say phrases like; I am grateful. I love making a difference. And, I can do all things through Christ who strengthens me.

*"Death and life are in the power of the tongue;
and they that love it shall eat
the fruit therefore."*
Proverbs 18:21

We work so much, it's also important to prioritize getting good rest. That's how we recharge. Recharge and energize your mind. Take a social media break and practice cyber silence for a few hours or an entire day. Turn off all of your electronics. If you can, get a massage. Do some journaling and writing in a gratitude journal. Put your thoughts on paper. How did you spend your day? How can you improve on it tomorrow?

Love Yourself

The practical physical routine of self-care each day should become a weekly activity. This doesn't have to be expensive but do something that makes you feel good about yourself. Take some time out to sit in the midst of the breezy air, take a bubble bath with candles, listen to soft, instrumental music. Set aside time to cozy up with a good read, while sipping on a tasteful blend of tea. Take yourself out for a nice romantic dinner, just you, loving yourself.

Another thing you may want to consider is self-love towards your body, and all of the amazing things it can do. Rather than looking at yourself in a way that is entirely appearance-oriented, view your body as a beautiful machine.

> *"I will praise You, for I am fearfully*
> *and wonderfully made;*
> *your works are wonderful;*
> *I know that full well."*
> Psalm 139:14

Every day you are capable of waking up and getting yourself out of bed. You are capable of hiking, running, taking long walks, or just walking around the block. You're capable of driving yourself to work. You can write, you can read. The tasks we perform on a daily basis should not be taken for granted. Do we have a perfect looking body? Of course not. But why should the way your body LOOKS be the entire basis of your happiness? What about the way your body performs? Is that not worthy of loving?

When you take a step back and look at yourself based on what you can DO and not just how you LOOK, not only does this "new view" give you a different perspective of yourself to love, it also motivates you to take better care of your temple (body). In order to do the amazing things your body does every day; it needs excellent care like any good machine. Your body deserves to be loved and nurtured to its fullest potential.

Lastly, on your journey to self-love, never base your worth on whether or not someone else is capable of loving you. Base your worth on whether or not YOU are capable of loving you. Base your worth on your ability to love others.

In life, you aren't going to be everyone's cup of tea. But, there's someone out there who's taste in tea is

Love Yourself

exactly what you have to offer. Until then, take care of yourself, and learn to be alone. Learn to be your own best friend, learn to love yourself unconditionally. Do the things that make you happy.

Love others. Live your best, most happy life and do it alone. And when the moment comes when you find someone worthy of your time, let them add to your happiness. Don't allow them to be your whole happiness.

We all want a perfect love story, but no one says that your love for yourself can't be the first and best love story you ever write.

CHAPTER SIX
EMBRACE GOD'S LOVE

"We often are overtaken by the destination and not appreciating the journey. The journey is what develops and establishes us. Countless stories are told of miners being trapped for days and hours beneath the underground, due to an avalanche or other unforeseen circumstances. Fortunately, the basic survival instinct kicks in. Little food or no food is available. The air is thin and almost nonexistent. Those on medication are without proper essentials for maintaining good health. Working together becomes a necessity, it's no longer an option. One disengaged miner could set-back the chances of rescue. While rescuers are working around the clock, just one wrong decision could destroy the operation of a successful rescue mission. Both the trapped miners and the rescuers are frantically living off of pure instinct, skill, and knowledge. Deprived of proper food and air, their minds are working on limited fuel, therefore decision-making is less clear and precise. Everyone is focusing on survival, while 'experiencing' an arduous 'journey.'"

—Linda G. Hodge

You've focused on the endgame, but are you also "experiencing" the journey? Do you believe with unrelenting conviction and confidence that Jesus loves you? Are you convinced that a fiery passion rage within Him toward you?

It's so much easier to believe He loves somebody else like that. But right now, this is about Jesus and you and nobody else. Everything starts here.

We cannot out-love Jesus because love is not just something He does. It's something He is. Every time you

Embrace God's Love

choose Him because He is pursuing you. Every time you have something to say to Him because He's saying something to you. Every time you choose Him, He has already chosen you.

Anytime you get up before dawn and head into your den to pray, He is already there waiting for you. You cannot beat Jesus to the punch. He's already there patiently waiting for you to enter into His presence. He is never distracted from you. Jesus does not feel the same way about you that you do. You may like yourself one minute and hate yourself the next but that's because you're not Jesus.

Neither am I. He's not moody. Thank God He is not subject to hormones.

> *"For the grace of God that brings*
> *Salvation has appeared to all people."*
> Titus 2:11

He knew your name before creation. He knew all your life would entail. Yes, He knew all about your dysfunctional family that would shape your world. And the hideous, tormenting thoughts that would chase you like a dog chasing his tail in an ever-circling motion.

Many of these tormenting thoughts have created a shame-based behavior within. The overabundant defensiveness and the times we overreacted to little things were mainly due to shame. If a family member would tell us we could do something differently or better, we would get defensive because they are telling us we are not good enough or didn't try hard enough. In reality, they didn't mean that at all. They were simply making a suggestion—and we would make a federal case out of it. A "shame" button in us got pushed, and in turn, our defensive reaction shames them. Then here we go again, apologizing for overreacting.

No authentic and long-lasting change occurs without God's help and the work of the Holy Spirit in a person's life. Committed and genuine spirituality is an essential foundation for believing in yourself. God begins with us where we are. We do not need to climb a ladder or tower to get to where He is. We do not have to have all our problems solved before we are worthy of calling on Him.

Embrace God's Love

Some of us, like myself, have been victims of sexual and physical abuse. The struggle to trust others is a result of the fear we have of being taken advantage of. It is the consequence of the normal human questions:

- Why would you do this to me?
- What did I do to deserve this?

There are almost universal family rules in dysfunctional families. They are:

- Don't Talk
- Don't Trust
- Don't Feel

There are grandmothers, and mothers who have taken secrets to the grave, because they refused to talk and instead offered harsh warnings: Don't trust anybody outside the family; Who knows what they might do or say about our family? Besides, their families are just like ours; and our family depends upon you—don't let us down. Don't Feel says, "if you don't allow yourself to think about the situation, it won't hurt so bad. After all, you really don't hurt that badly.

When a child shuts down his painful, emotional side, he also loses the ability to express his joyous side. Emotions act as a whole.

Some families actually use statements that squelch emotions, "If you don't quit crying, I'll give you something to cry about! Children should be seen and not heard. You'll get over it. Be tough—it will happen many times, so get used to it." I remember my Mom repeatedly telling my older sister, "Giiirrrlll, the police is going to have to come and get me off of you."

A family should be a communal environment where its members can count on the safe assurance of others to fuel emotional needs. This nurturing environment should be a "filling station," where needs for love are met so that its members have the strength to go out and interact with the world and accomplish the heavenly Father's command to "subdue" and "rule" the world (Genesis 1:28). The need for love and interaction is met through; Warm moments of telling stories and saying prayers at bedtime; In-depth conversations at the dinner table about the day's events; and Moments of sharing painful hurts at work or

Embrace God's Love

at school, and of having tears wiped away. Such times for assurance means that no matter how hard things are in the outside world, at home everything is OK. There should be precious moments when parents are vulnerable and thereby letting their children know that parents are human, too.

Sadly, we have learned to cope with life in an unhealthy way. Why don't we just do it right, and embrace God's love?

Many are confused about God's perception of His children: God thinks I am all bad, God hates me for my failures and will punish me; His grace does not apply to me. God expects me to be further along than I am able to be at this time; He forgets that sanctification is a process.

Others are confused about themselves: If I am not perfect, I am worse than everyone else. If I am immature, something is wrong with me. If I fail, I am defective. If I am unable, there is no hope for me.

The problem is we have learned to hide. This hiding began with Adam and Eve in the Garden when they first became aware that they were no longer perfect. They hid (Genesis 3:7-10), and we have been hiding ever since. Here's the problem with hiding: nothing grows in the dark. It's time to walk out of the dark, into His marvelous light. God's love toward us is unfailing.

> *"For God so loved the world that He gave His only begotten Son."*
> John 3:16

God knew your name before creation. He knew what all your life would entail. He knew both strands of your DNA by heart. He appointed the color of your eyes and the prints of your fingers. He chose the generation in which you'd live and planted you in an exact spot on the planet to initiate divine purpose. He enacted a plan of epic proportions that would include you. His Son took on flesh for all humankind, yes. But that includes you. He gave His life for you. He rose from the dead for you. He sits at the right hand of God to intercede for you. He sent His promised Holy Spirit to seal, sanctify, thrill, and fill you.

Jesus pursues you every single day. Jesus valiantly fights for you every single day. Every single day, He gazes on your face and brings you one step closer to seeing His face.

Embrace God's Love

Do you have the audacity to take what He's done personally? Do you have the audacity to believe to your bones that He boldly pursued you with His passion?

We'll never be freed up to **Embrace His Love** if we're living our lives as one big shameless apology. To get where you and I are headed, we're going to have to recognize how much He loves us, and **Embrace His love.**

Things that aren't dead don't stay buried. If we suppress our insecurities rather than inviting specific truth to supplant them, we leave ourselves wide open of not **Embracing His Love**. The result is a constant psychological roller coaster. We can feel generally secure and on the right track one moment then get completely derailed and go off the cliff the next.

Here's the good news: we don't have to go off the cliff. We can choose to have a different reaction. Choosing a different reaction leads to a new feeling, and the new feeling leads to more consistent reactions. The result? We won't get derailed.

One of the most common human claims is that we can't change the way we feel. That may be true, but we can change the way we think, which will change the way we act. And as we change the way we act, the way we feel also begins to change.

We will always have triggers of insecurity, but we get to decide whether or not we're going to take the bait.

If you're like me, these may be refreshing new revelations for you:

- You can be hurt without also being insecure.
- You can be disappointed without also being insecure.
- You can be shocked without also being insecure.
- You can have doubts without also being insecure.
- You can even be humbled without also being insecure.

Insecurity is more than a complex emotion. It is a lie about our God sanctioned condition. While something may cause us to feel sad, confused, angry, or threatened, we have the power to choose whether or not it gets to assault our security and the ability to **Embrace God's Love**.

"I belong I am my love and his desire is for me."
Song of Solomon (7:10)

Embrace God's Love

Try starting your day with that verse every morning. Look at that woman in the bathroom mirror who wonders if she possesses anything worth wanting. And, say those words out loud to her. Say them like you mean it! And if, for whatever reason, you need the verse in the worst way—whether loneliness, loss, abandonment, or rejection—write it on an index card and tape it to the edge of your mirror, where you can see it every time you see yourself.

CHAPTER SEVEN
DISCOVER YOUR BEST

"In gold mining, panning is really a simple method of separating particles of gold from soil or gravels by washing in a pan with water. The typical pan used is a light, rugged, circular metal dish with a flat bottom and sides that slope out about 45°. The inner surface of the dish must be smooth and free from grease and rust. In panning for gold from streams, the pan is first filled halfway or so with gravel, soil, and rocks from places where the current is slower. The pan is then immersed in the water, and the mixture is thoroughly moistened and stirred. This allows the lumps of clay to be broken up, and large stones are picked out."

—Linda G. Hodge

God has divinely engineered us for our purpose in life. He is expecting us to emerge!! The enemy is after our purpose. If my purpose is unknown my life is likened to a ship sailing in the ocean without any direction. Without its compass, a ship is lost.

Because we matter, the enemy is terrified of a woman who is clear about her purpose and confident in her mission.

There isn't a single individual that is born without a purpose. It shouldn't be something that we accidentally, mysteriously become aware of. Many people go to the grave without discovering their purpose. While others second-guess, doubt, and self-sabotage themselves, and never step into fully embracing their best, their purpose.

Your purpose consists of the central motivating aims of your life—the reasons you get up in the morning. Purpose can guide life decisions, influence behavior, shape goals, offer direction, and create meaning.

Discover Your Best

Purpose is not merely an occupation. It shows up in everything you do. Its why God needs you. It's why you're here.

And then, there are your gifts. Everyone has a gift, something unique to her. We can use this gift to better ourselves and to better the lives of others. Gifts are your God-given endowments, abilities, and attributes that improve the lives of others. Your gifts clarify your purpose. So often we try to bury our gifts, and society encourages it. When that happens, our gifts remain unused, and that's sad. We have to make the effort to discover our gifts!

How can you discover your gifts? You start by becoming self-aware. You get to know who you are and what you have within you. We have all been given a gift. Something specifically God has given to us to affect mankind.

Have you done a life audit?

Just like an accountant audits a company's books, you can perform an audit of your life. In the business world, there are internal audits and external audits. An internal audit involves a company's own accountant looking at its books. An external audit means an independent accountant comes in to perform the audit. You can apply the same principle to your life. You can perform an internal audit by taking inventory of who you are and working to understand yourself better. What are your priorities? What do you like? What don't you like? What are you good at? What are you not so good at?

Part of the value of performing an internal audit is that you get an understanding of where you are currently. It's extremely hard to go somewhere else if you don't know the location of your starting point. There's nobody better equipped for performing your internal audit than you. Ask yourself what you do and don't like. What affects you powerfully?

Then you can go on to do an external audit. This involves asking other people about their perceptions of you. Choose people you respect, whose opinions you value, and who have spent a lot of time with you. Make sure you choose people who will be sincere. Ask them to think about your best qualities and areas where you need to make some improvements. Then, ask them to tell you what they think.

Take what you hear and match it up with what you discovered during your internal audit. Look at both audits and find themes that continually show up. What do you notice? How can you take action from what you learned?

If we expect to go "all-in" with our purpose and gifts, we must; get out of our way, be willing to take the journey alone, become unstoppable, risk failure, focus on one area at a time, and recognize what authentic success means to you.

In addition, you must discover your strengths. Your strengths can show up in many forms. First, there's talent, which we are born with. Then there are skills, which are learned and practiced. There's also strength obtained from learning and gaining knowledge. All of these elements come together to form your personal strengths.

Look for **SIGNS** of your strengths.

> **Success:** What have you done really well in the past? What do you do that almost always gets great results?

> **Instinct:** What comes naturally to you? What kinds of things, when you do them, seem to

happen almost automatically? What are you naturally drawn to?

Learning Skills: What do you love so much that you pick up new knowledge on the topic effortlessly? What are you so fascinated by that constant learning and practicing is a pleasure and not a chore?

Needs: What do you feel satisfied by doing? What do you feel drawn to, to the point where it feels like you need to do it in order to feel complete?

Almost as important as our relationship with God is our relationship with ourselves. It's easy to elevate others over ourselves. Therefore, you have to shift making YOU an important person in your life, not an afterthought. In order to discover your best, you must:

1. Stop minimizing and devaluing who you are.
2. Clear your mind of all self-defeating thoughts.
3. Eliminate the need for validation from others.

Discover Your Best

In short, you must love, honor, and believe in yourself. You must put yourself first in all matters—make your true self a priority. Putting yourself first means speaking your truth with firmness and boldness. It means understanding that "No" is a complete sentence. It's an answer you are entitled to deploy when you need it.

Only by having a mature, loving, respectful relationship with yourself can you have meaningful relationships with others. It's time to rebuild your long-lost relationship with yourself.

1. What do you like about you?
2. What are five things you appreciate about yourself?
3. When do you feel the most vulnerable?
4. What do you do to "protect" yourself during times of vulnerability?
5. What habits do you need to break that will empower you to live more truthfully, and with more self-respect in your relationship with yourself?

All the great things God has put inside us—our purpose, gifts, dreams, plans, and talents—are all Satan's targets. He is afraid of men and women who have faith in God's wisdom and power, because they take their visions and translate them into action. They not only set goals; they make them happen.

The deceiver fears the treasure we possess. His destructive tactics and deceptive influences come into our lives to nullify and entrap all God has given to us. He isn't going to let us fulfill our purpose without encountering resistance from him.

> *"Guard the good deposits that was entrusted to you—guard it with the Help of the Holy Spirit who lives in us."*
> 2 Timothy 1:14

One way you can prepare to defend your purpose is to make wise choices. Consider carefully with whom you associate and where you spend your time. Be cautious with whom you share your dreams—if you share them at all.

A second way to defend your purpose is to fortify yourself against the assaults of the enemy. You must seek God's discipline and direction in your life.

Discover Your Best

God gave you your potential—your gifts, talents, abilities, energies, creativity, ideas, aspirations, and dreams—for the blessing of others. You bear the responsibility for activating, releasing, and maximizing everything as a deposit for the next generation.

The next generation needs what you have. Don't be a generational thief. That's why it's so important that you discover what you were born to be, then do it. Fulfill your own personal purpose for the glory of God. Your obedience to God's will and purpose for your life is a personal decision, but not a private one. God has designed the universe in such a way that the purpose of all mankind is interdependent; your purpose affects millions.

Suppose Mary had aborted Jesus, or Andrew had failed to introduce Peter to Jesus. What if Abraham had not left the Land of Ur, or Joseph had refused to go to Egypt. These examples show that although our obedience is always a personal decision, it is never a private matter.

Don't rob the next generation of your contribution. It's time to "Discover Your Best."

CHAPTER EIGHT
GET OUT OF YOUR FEELINGS

"While the pan is still underwater, it is then given a combination of shaking and gyratory motion. This allows the heavy particles to settle and brings the lighter material to the surface. At intervals, the pan is tilted, and the light surface material is washed off. This process is continued until only heavy 'black sands' and gold remains. The material is dried and the gold removed. Panning is slow, backbreaking work. But experienced hands result in little to no loss of gold."

—Linda G. Hodge

MATTERS OF THE HEART

It's time to live your life with no limits! You can go further than you believe and accomplish more than you dream.

We are responsible for the limits we put on ourselves. Limits can be traced when we form and accept a belief. "I can't do math," and for many of us that belief continues today. All of us place limits on ourselves. Fortunately, we don't have to be limited by our false limitations.

Most of us have established these limited beliefs by needing approval from others. Do you ever ask why you feel the need to do things to please others rather than yourself? It all starts with self-esteem (or lack of it). Some of the factors relate to your natural personality, while others stem from external influences such as your upbringing, cultural and/or educational background. The list goes on.

I can totally relate. Unconsciously, I downplayed or altered my own behavior or opinions in favor of someone else's. Afraid to say 'no' for fear of disapproval is a HUGE one. The end result of this behavior is to run yourself ragged—ultimately resenting all the things you've committed yourself to doing.

Get Out Of Your Feelings

Not standing up for your own rights, thereby being a human doormat, is a common trait when you don't realize your value.

Living in a limiting environment is another factor of adopting limited beliefs also. Too many people simply accept whatever environment they're born into. They think it's normal, and they start to believe they don't have any other choices in life. When that happens, they've created a self-imposed limit on their life.

If I look back and think about what I went through in lessening the grit of limited beliefs, the most prevalent shift occurred when I was exposed to a way of thinking that I wasn't accustomed to.

Exposure can be such a gift.

You may be facing challenges. Others may not believe in you. You may have had a tough past. That doesn't take away what you possess or your future success.

You can be successful if others don't believe in you, but you cannot be successful if you don't believe in yourself. And to make a change, you must take action and do the right things that will allow you to possess self-belief.

MATTERS OF THE HEART

I want to help you believe in yourself, and give you a path forward to increasing your capacity. I want to help you make the most of whatever potential you possess. Do you constantly dwell on the way your life has evolved until now? Let it go. It doesn't matter. Write a new chapter of your life. Take control and truly narrate this new chapter of your life.

I consciously work toward not making emotional decisions. Sometimes it works favorably, while other times I find myself at the mercy of my emotions getting the best of me.

Furthermore, emotional capacity is significant to personal growth and success. However, not enough discussion or recognition is spent on understanding how to control "agents of depletion" from draining one's emotional capacity. Your capacity to properly process emotions is significant to your success.

Emotional capacity is the ability to handle adversity, failure, criticism, change, and pressure in a positive way. I've found that the inability to deal with stress or emotional pressure takes a lot out of people. They give up, break down, or do unhealthy things to try to escape the pressure. I've had first- hand, close-up observations seeing my mother have a stroke at the age of 61, then later passing at the age of 68. Her primary symptom was hypertension, but the root cause was stress related. The way you handle stress hinges on not having emotional capacity to deal with the pressures of life.

I want to share with you seven practices that I've observed people with high emotional capacity exhibit. I'm actively adopting these successful behaviors in my life:

1. Emotionally Strong Women Are Proactive in Dealing with Their Emotions

The first and maybe most important thing that emotionally strong people do is take an active approach to their emotions. They never say, "That's just how I feel. I can't help that. I keep it real." They are never victims of their own feelings.

I'm not sure that I will ever be the "master of my emotions," but I will always get in motion to try to slow the steam engine down.

2. Emotionally Strong Women Do Not Waste Time Feeling Sorry for Themselves

The way you deal with difficulties and avoid feeling sorry for yourself can be as unique as you are. I'm working toward asking myself this question before the emotional fuses begin to rise. "What is the worst that can happen?" If you can ask yourself that question and then prepare to accept it, you can hit a good "recovery shot." If it's as bad as the worst possible outcome, then you can deal with it.

3. Emotionally Strong Women Do Not Allow Others to Control Their Relationships

Relationships are complicated and can be difficult to navigate. One of the ways you can keep proper control of your life and not allow others to take that control is to understand that you wear different hats in life; wife, mother, friend, leader, sister, daughter, and businessperson. The hat you have on determines the way you interact in the relationship.

4. Emotionally Strong Women Do Not Waste Energy on Things They Cannot Control

As each year passes, I'm learning to control what I can and not waste energy on what I can't control. This is one of the most important lessons we can learn in life.

Emotionally strong people don't waste their energy when they are stuck in bad traffic, lose their luggage, or get caught in a storm. They recognize that all of these factors are beyond their control. Instead, they focus on what they can control.

5. Emotionally Strong Women Do Not Keep Making the Same Mistakes

It's been said that the definition of insanity is doing the same thing over and over but expecting different results. When we think about it logically, we should expect the same results from the same actions. Yet, many people find themselves in ruts doing what they've always done but wishing for something different. How exhausting! Why does it happen? Because they never take the time to stop, and figure out why they are getting the same results.

6. Emotionally Strong Women Don't Allow the Highs or Lows to Control Their Lives

You have to limit the impact of both the highs and lows. Whether you are experiencing a high or low don't marinate on it more than 24 hours. Rejoicing too long may cause you to become too comfortable and lose the desire to move on to your next assignment. If you are experiencing a low, take a mental break. Regroup, Re-engage, and Replenish. After 24 hours, stop grieving and take off the black.

7. Emotionally Strong Women Understand, Appreciate, and Grow Through Their Struggle

Many people resist change but want immediate results, while hoping for a life void of problems. Life involves struggle. Emotionally strong women expect difficulties and learn to appreciate the growth they bring.

They don't expect immediate results. Knowing they are in for the long haul, they put on patience. They know it's perfectly fine to try new things and fail. They run into obstacles but persevere. They keep going, keep working. They focus on the right decisions they need to make, and make them quickly.

EMOTIONAL CAPACITY QUESTIONS

1. In the past, have you considered yourself to be emotionally strong or emotionally weak as a person? Explain.

2. Which of the seven practices of emotional strong women best describes your approach?

3. Which of the seven practices of emotionally strong women is most difficult for you and why? What could you do to improve in that area?

ABOUT THE AUTHOR

Linda G. Hodge, is a wife, mother, grandmother, great grandmother. She is an accomplished entrepreneur, author, and compelling motivational speaker. Linda Hodge creates and produces conferences, seminars, and extreme makeovers, designed to equip, support, and empower women to walk in their Divine destiny.

She has authored five books: *Woman Under Construction, Woman Under Construction Tool Book, Winning in Life: How to Bounce Back from Adversity, 52 Questions and Answers for Singles,* and *Bruised But Not Broken.*

Linda Hodge has been married to Dr. Fred Hodge for more than 38 years. Together they co-pastor Living

Praise Christian Church with campuses in both the San Fernando and Antelope Valleys in Southern California, and co-founders of Transformation Mentoring Culture. As a life coach for women, she helps women break free from a mindset of procrastination by identifying roadblocks and negative thought patterns. It helps them shift their lives and priorities so they can live in full Divine purpose.

Her testimony is that God has a restoration plan for all those who have been broken, hurt, displaced, or abused.

You can follow Linda G. Hodge on Facebook, WOVEN 21-Day Shift or visit her website, lindaghodge.com.

Linda G. Hodge is a firm believer that what is within you is greater than anything in your surroundings.